FOR THE LOVE OF A
BLOB FISH

By

One Old Grandpa

I would like to dedicate this book to Nadine a girl with such a love for all things that of all the animals and creatures in the world; her favorite is the blob fish. If only more of us loved like this what a wonderful world this would be. ☺

O' Yah that's the spot, just keep rubbing

Above is Nadine working with a dog that was rescued. I pray the Lord continues to give you the joys of your heart as you give love and compassion to those in need.

Tale of a Blob Fish . . .

Deep, deep beneath the oceans depths, hidden from the eyes or mortal man lives a creature, that, though it has never seen man nor have many men ever seen it, bares a striking similarity to the face of men. This creature is called, "The Blob Fish."

The above picture is of a young, not fully developed blob fish. Notice how smooth its features are? Surprisingly in this state it looks like most of the other fish in the deep waters of the ocean. This is the true nature and shape of the

blob fish. Though they look quite ugly when removed from the safety of the deep waters they look normal, like the above fish in their natural habitat.

Many people find blob fish to be quite beautiful in appearance. But there are more that seem prejudiced against them than are for them. Notice the wonderful pink hue radiating from the blob fish below.

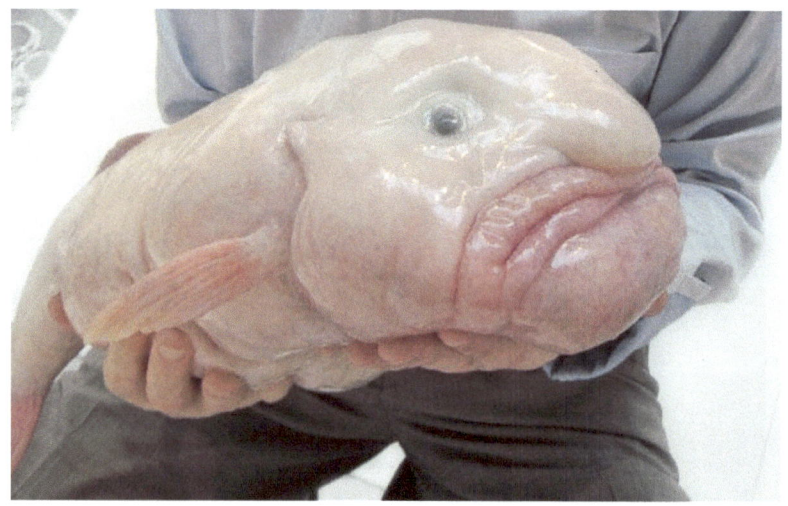

One point of interest is this: In 2013 the blob fish was voted the, "ugliest creature in the world." I don't know about you but I think it is kind of very cute looking.

Strange and fun facts . . .

Did you know that not all fish can swim? The blob fish is one of them. Because of its composition and build it does not swim, it floats. This may seem to be strange. It may even seem to be inefficient but actually the opposite is true. The blob fish is perfectly designed for life on the bottom of the ocean. It floats around the bottom like a type of fishy vacuum cleaner. The blob fish allows the underwater currents to move it around just above the floor of the ocean. It then opens it mouth and eats everything that floats in front of its mouth. So you see it is like an underwater vacuum.

Could you imagine what life would be like without bones or an inner structure to support your bodies frame? Your body would be nothing more than a gelatinous compilation of skin, muscle and cartilage. You would be like the blob fish. Burt thinks that would be funny. Now that's a set of choppers that would make any dentist proud. Actually that is a photo shopped picture. Blob fish do not have teeth like that but it does look funny.

The favorite foods of the blob fish are crustaceans such as crayfish, crabs, lobsters, shrimp and krill.

Here is something interesting about blob fish; they are similar to water in density. Scientist classifies the blob fish as being a gelatinous mass. This is the reason why blob fish change shape and appearance when removed from the high pressure depths of the sea. It is the under water pressure of the depths that keep the blob fish looking like a normal fish. The body of the blob fish has a density slightly less than water which makes it perfectly suited for floating along the ocean floor. It literally lives a life of leisure. Here are some blob fish facts.

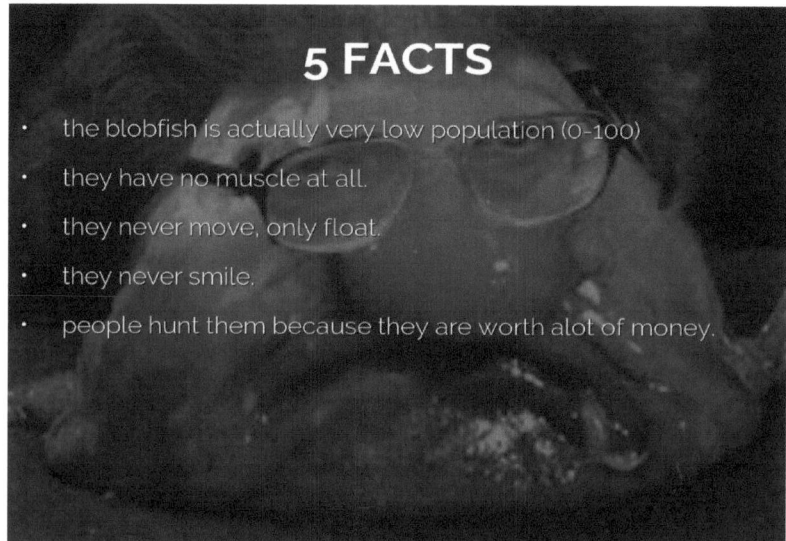

5 FACTS

- the blobfish is actually very low population (0-100)
- they have no muscle at all.
- they never move, only float.
- they never smile,
- people hunt them because they are worth alot of money.

Few in number and counting down . . .

So far oceanographers and fisherman have only found the blob fish in three areas; Australia, New Zealand and Tasmania. They seem to be almost entirely indigenous to the coastlines of Australia. Notice how Australia is completely surrounded by water.

Blob fish do not have an ability to hunt or seek prey; they are entirely dependent upon the currents that carry them along just above the ocean's floor. This sound great and it would be but for one problem; because they cannot swim they do not have the ability to evade or escape from *predators and of course man is the greatest of all the sea's predators. Here is a picture of a blob fish that was caught in a fishing trolley's dragnet.*

Blob fish have no natural form of defense nor escape so unlike most other fish or crustaceans they do not have the ability to evade capture. This has created a very bad situation for both blob fish and deep sea fisherman. Let me explain. Take a look at the picture below.

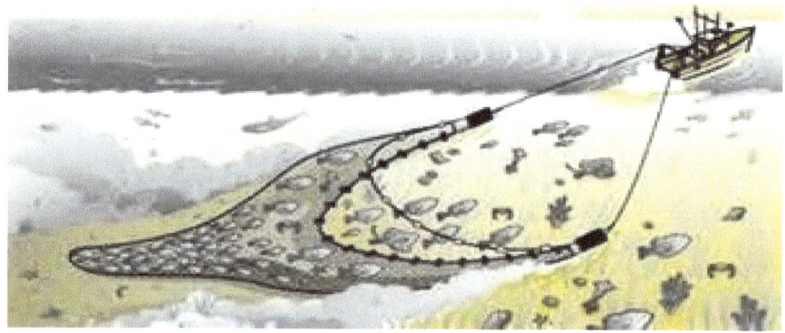

The above picture is of a deep sea trawler. As you can see the net simply scoops up everything in its path. Blob fish are usually caught in these bottom trawling nets. Trawling nets are huge nets that drag just off of the bottom of the oceans floor. Realize that the fishermen do not intentionally try to catch the blob fish, they are bycatch. The fishing industry calls any fish or creature that is not caught intentionally but rather by accident, bycatch. Here is where the conflict occurs. The blob fish are an endangered species of fish with no ability to evade the deep sea nets. Actually the nets create an inner current that pulls the blob fish into the net; there are not able to avoid being caught. Here is another example.

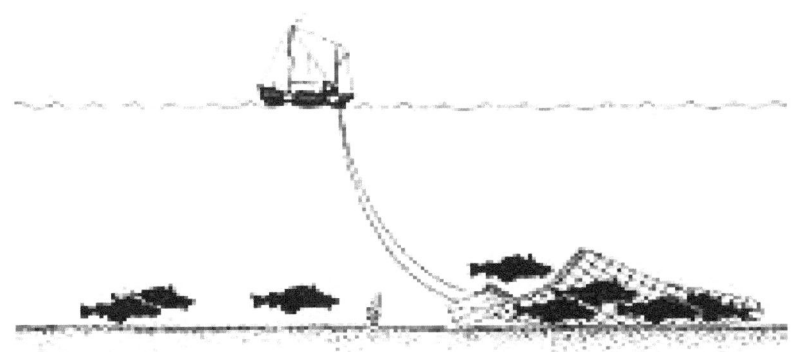

Deep sea trawlers amass great quantities of various harvests. These fisherman and their families depend upon them harvesting as much from the oceans floor as possible. Everything is scooped up from lobster to crabs to large and small fish of every deep water type.

Cause of great concern . . .

This type of fishing has scientists very concerned. They believe that such types of fishing have placed the blob fish into the endangered species category. As of right now we do not have enough information on the blob fish to make proper recommendations or to enact better procedure.

Blob fish are not a common fish, even in the waters around Australia. The oceans are massive and vast. Strangely we know more about outer space than we do about the earth's seas and oceans. Here are some of the things that we do know about blob fish.

The population of blob fish is estimated to be less than 100. This is why they have been placed on the endangered species list. It is still unknown how they reproduce but it has been observed that the female will lay thousands of tiny pink eggs on the ocean floor. Then the male will sit over them until they hatch. It is speculated that the male fertilizes the eggs from this position after they are laid by the female. This is the only way to preserve the eggs since there is no vegetation nor *caves or crevices to hide the eggs from predators. Here is a picture of a pair of blob fish.*

The female is the one on the bottom getting ready to lay her eggs. Even though the oceans floor is very dark, light is mostly absent at this depth, you can see how beautifully pink the pair are. What is even more interesting is that the eggs will be colored just like the parents, a beautiful pink hue.

Blob fish seem to be a communal fish. It has been observed that several females will all gather next to each other to lay their eggs. Scientists watched four different female blob fish make nests next to each other and were amazed when they saw just how many eggs they laid. They estimated that the four females lay over 100,000 eggs! That is incredible! One question that scientists are trying to answer is; "if the blob fish lay so many eggs why are there not more of them?" They believe the answer lies in the deep sea trawling. It is believed that when a deep sea net crosses over a nest of blob fish that it scoops up all the males and females in one pass. This leaves the remaining eggs defenseless and if there is one thing that other fish and crustaceans like it is fish eggs.

Here is an interesting point. Male blob fish will hover over the eggs fanning the eggs with their bodies. Scientist believes this keeps the eggs from being covered and damaged by sand or other floating debris. It would appear that blob fish are a very maternal and paternal species of fish with both parents protecting and caring for the unborn young. This means they are a very loving type of fish.

Blob fish are very deep . . .

If you wanted to find a blob fish you would have to go down pretty deep in order to find one. They have been found at depths as shallow as 2,000 feet and depths as deep as 3,900 feet. The most common depth is 2,700 feet. Now, that is incredibly deep! The estimated pressure at that depth is 1169 pound per square inch. The water pressure at that depth is very great. It would instantly crush a normal human! But due to the lack of density of the blob fish's body it thrives at those depths. It is when you bring it up into shallower waters or take it out of the water that it is unable to survive.

While the blob fish is in deep water it maintains a normal appearance. But if you bring it up to less dense water something strange happens to it; a very drastic change occurs. It loses the pressure that maintains its forma and life. It is the lack of all that water pressure that causes the blob fish to blow up into the distorted appearance that resemblance a fat faced human. But do not despair even a blob fish out of water can look appealing.

Look at Burt below. Here is one fine gentleman of a blob fish, (if that is possible).

He, he, he, now that's funny! Burt really doesn't look like that. I just thought it would be funny to dress him up like an Aristocrat. I hope you liked it.

He does look kind of good in the top hat and eye glass. The bow tie and moustache add certain elegance to his demeanor; don't you think?

Well enough kidding around, this is what a blow fish really looks like out of the water.

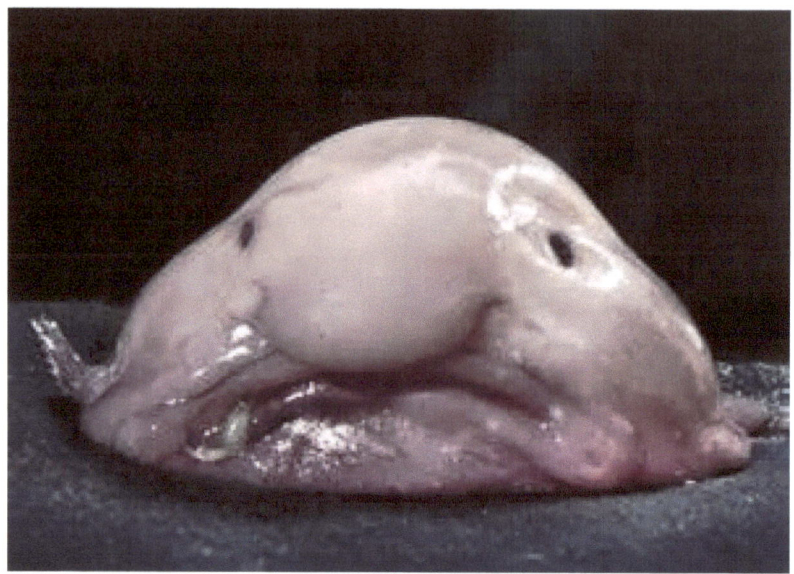

This distorted image is the result of coming apart at the seams. Bringing a blob fish up and out of the water is very cruel and painful to the blob fish resulting in its death.

Many times people have asked the question; "can a blob fish live in a tank?" "Can it be kept as a pet?" The answer to both questions is yes. The blob fish can survive in a tank and kept as a pet but there would have to be some condition met.

The first thing to realize is that the blob fish would have to be captured underwater at its natural depth and then placed into a special tank that would maintain the proper water pressure for it. Then it would have to be transported to a facility with the proper equipment and high pressure tanks capable of duplicating the blob fish's natural environment. Because the blob fish is used to a dark environment it needs to be shielded from normal light so if it was transported to a holding facility it would have to be kept in an almost completely dark atmosphere. To date no blob fish has even been captured alive. They have all died before being pulled from the water. The blob fish is a beautiful fish that can only be enjoyed through pictures or deep sea diving apparatus.

Sadly when blob fish are pulled from the sea it is a complete waste of both life and resource. Blob fish are an inedible fish. When they are pulled from the water they transform into a bland, gelatinous blob with near water consistency. What are left are the disfigured remains of what was once a very beautiful fish. It seems for the better part of a century deep sea trawlers have been scooping up this beautiful species of fish, only to kill them and destroy the nests which hold the potential for continuation and propagation of the *species known as Psychrolutes, (that is its Scientific classification name). They are also known as "Fathead Sculpins." Here is a side view of this amazing species.*

The above specimen is from a research expedition called, "The NORFANZ Expedition." The Norfanz expedition was launched in 2003 to conduct research in the Northwest of New Zealand. This specimen was captured and preserved in alcohol. Isn't it interesting how when it is preserved it looks as normal as any other fish?

In 2013 the blob fish was adopted as the official mascot of the, "Ugly Animal Preservation Society." Man what an honor. But as ugly as the blob fish is that honor is only deserved for them after they have died. As you have seen from the photos, living blob fish are quite beautiful and very passionate fish. They are not only communal, living in groups, but once they form mating pairs the male and female are completely devoted to working together in caring for their future young. Here are some more pictures of blob fish.

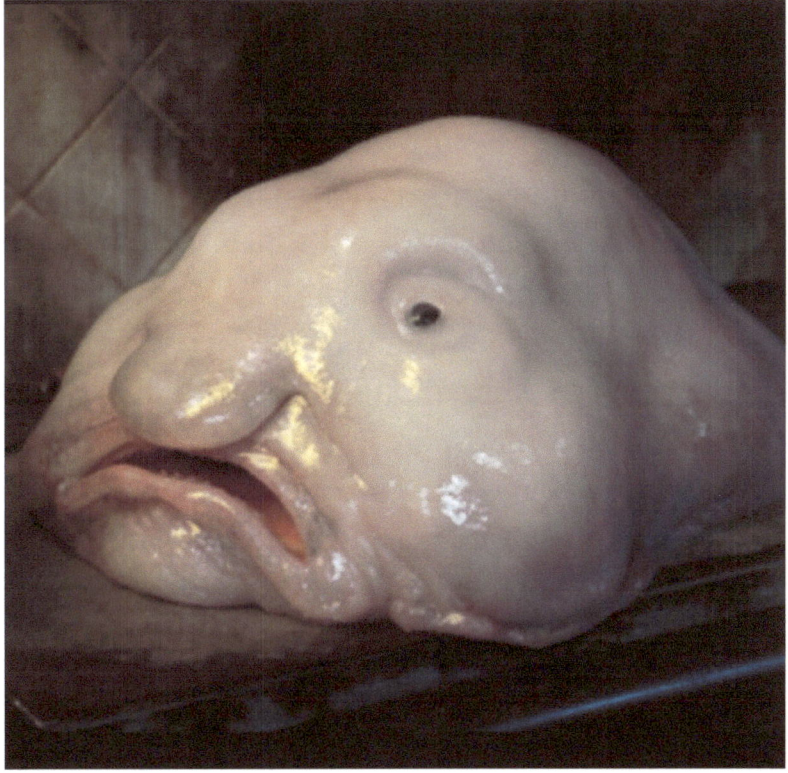

From all appearance it would seem that the blob fish has teeth but that is not the case. It's mouth does not possess any bone, it is all soft, pliable flesh. Scientists are still trying to figure out how they are able to eat the crustaceans that they do. It is proposed that they swallow the prey whole and the digestive juices in their stomach break down whatever they have eaten allowing them to absorb all of the potential nutrients and minerals. Scientists are still unsure as to whether the blob fish even goes to the bathroom like other fish. There are many speculations about this wondrous fish. Because of its inability for easy access for research the process of discovery about the blob fish and its habits is very, very slow. There is so much to be discovered but scientists are very hopeful. As technology and research advance the prospects of learning more about this strange and exotic fish are very promising. I will finish this volume with some more pictures of blob fish. I hope you have enjoyed learning about the blob fish as much as I have in researching and writing on it. Now off to the pictures. ☺

The picture on the next page is a high resolution photo shot from a depth above 3,200 feet below sea level.

See how truly beautiful the blog fish is? Also you can see why it is classified as a fathead sculpin. It is believed that the blob fish was created with a fathead and a small body to that it could much more easily inhale prey that floats by. Remember it does not have the ability to hunt or swim but due to its density, simply floats like a fishy vacuum cleaner on the bottom.

Here is a picture of the ugliest of all mascots.

For such an ugly mug, the blog fish are a celebrated species.

Notice the delicious blog fish cupcakes below. Mmmm, mmm! I would love to eat one of those.

I particularly love sprinkles. Let's see what kind of picture awaits your curiosity on the next page. ☺

Here is another funny picture.

I have no words for the picture below. I am a big fan of both grumpy cat and the blob fish.

One last shot, enjoy:

The End

www.ingramcontent.com/pod-product-compliance
Lightning Source LLC
Chambersburg PA
CBHW050927290526
45792CB00002B/917